Numbers

'Is God's promised redemption really unstoppable, even if the people of God disintegrates spiritually? This wonderful little devotional from Chris Wright will really make the book of Numbers come alive for you. And, as you will discover, the answer is a resounding "Yes"!'
Marcus Honeysett, Executive Director, Living Leadership

'If the book of Numbers is a bit of a blank in your mental map of the Bible, then this is a great place to start. Thirty short readings unfold its message, point us to Christ and connect to our lives. Again and again we see how God preserves his people despite our unfaithfulness. The result is comfort and hope built on the rock-solid grounds of God's promises and his mercy.'
Tim Chester, Pastor of Grace Church, Boroughbridge, North Yorkshire, a faculty member of Crosslands Training, Chair of Keswick Ministries and the author of over forty books, including Bible Matters: Meeting God in His Word *in the Keswick Foundations series*

30-DAY DEVOTIONAL

Numbers

Christopher Wright
with Elizabeth McQuoid

FOOD
FOR THE
JOURNEY

INTER-VARSITY PRESS
36 Causton Street, London SW1P 4ST, England
Email: ivp@ivpbooks.com
Website: www.ivpbooks.com

First published 2018

British Library Cataloguing-in-Publication Data
A catalogue record for this book is available from the British Library.

ISBN: 978–1–78359–720–8
eBook ISBN: 978–1–78359–721–5

Set in Avenir 11/15pt
Typeset in Great Britain by CRB Associates, Potterhanworth, Lincolnshire
Printed in Great Britain by CPI Group (UK) Ltd, Croydon, CR0 4YY

*Inter-Varsity Press publishes Christian books that are true to the Bible and that communicate
the gospel, develop discipleship and strengthen the church for its mission in the world.*

*IVP originated within the Inter-Varsity Fellowship, now the Universities and Colleges
Christian Fellowship, a student movement connecting Christian Unions in universities and
colleges throughout Great Britain, and a member movement of the International Fellowship
of Evangelical Students. Website: www.uccf.org.uk. That historic association is maintained,
and all senior IVP staff and committee members subscribe to the UCCF Basis of Faith.*

Preface

Can you guess how many sermons have been preached from the Keswick platform? Almost 6,500!

For over 140 years, the Convention in the English Lake District has welcomed gifted expositors from all over the world. Our archive is a treasure trove of sermons preached on every book of the Bible.

This series is an invitation to mine that treasure. It takes talks from the Bible Reading series given by well-loved Keswick speakers, past and present, and reformats them into daily devotionals. Where necessary the language has been updated but, on the whole, it is the message you would have heard had you been listening in the tent on Skiddaw Street. Each day of the devotional ends with a fresh section of application designed to help you apply God's Word to your own life and situation.

Whether you are a Convention regular or have never been to Keswick, this Food for the Journey series is a unique opportunity to study the Scriptures with a Bible teacher by your side. Each book was designed to fit in your jacket pocket or handbag so you can read it anywhere – over the breakfast table, on the commute into work or college, while you are waiting in your car, over your lunch break or in bed at night. Wherever life's journey takes you, time in God's Word is vital nourishment for your spiritual journey.

Our prayer is that these devotionals become your daily feast, a nourishing opportunity to meet with God through his Word. Read, meditate, apply and pray through the Scriptures given for each day, and allow God's truths to take root and transform your life.

If these devotionals whet your appetite for more, there is a 'For further study' section at the end of each book. You can also visit our website <www.keswickministries.org/resources> to find the full range of books, study guides, CDs, DVDs and mp3s available. Why not order an audio recording of the Bible Reading series to accompany your daily devotional?

Let the word of Christ dwell in you richly.
(Colossians 3:16, ESV)

Introduction
Numbers

Is God faithful?

The children of Israel were first-hand witnesses of God's amazing faithfulness. He had led them out of slavery in Egypt and opened up the Red Sea for them to cross. By Numbers chapter 10, the Israelites were about to leave Mount Sinai and God was with them: 'By day the pillar of cloud did not fail to guide them on their path, nor the pillar of fire by night to shine on the way they were to take. You gave your good Spirit to instruct them' (Nehemiah 9:19–20).

The future looked bright. Yet, despite all the evidence of God's faithfulness, the rest of the book of Numbers is a catalogue of grumbling, in-fighting and rebellion by God's ungrateful people. Instead of embracing freedom, they longed for the food they ate in slavery and wanted to return to Egypt (chapter 11). There was division at the very heart of the nation's leadership, and factions emerged jockeying for status and ambition, with complete disregard for humility or holiness (chapters 12 and 16). Fear and unbelief stoked rebellion among the people, and they refused to enter Canaan (chapters 13–14).

Such rebellion was not without its consequences. God took the people at their word and a whole generation died in the wilderness, never setting foot in the Promised Land. However, despite these repeated failures, God remained faithful. He even used the pagan seer, Balaam, to affirm his determination to bring Israel to the land of promise, highlighting in glorious technicolour that his blessing on Israel rested not on her faithfulness but on his sovereign will (chapters 22–24).

Like the Israelites, God's people still fail him and test his patience. But nothing – not our sin, the circumstances of our lives, nor the anti-Christian agenda growing in the West – will thwart God's redemptive plan. Though we face danger, suffering and even death, we can be sure of God's ultimate protection and eternal blessings.

These selected readings from the book of Numbers testify to God's faithfulness and invite us to trust him for today and all our tomorrows.

Day 1

Read Numbers 10:11–13, 29–36
Key verses: Numbers 10:29–31

....

> ²⁹Now Moses said to Hobab son of Reuel the Midianite, Moses' father-in-law, 'We are setting out for the place about which the Lᴏʀᴅ said, "I will give it to you." Come with us and we will treat you well, for the Lᴏʀᴅ has promised good things to Israel.' ³⁰He answered, 'No, I will not go . . .' ³¹But Moses said, 'Please do not leave us. You know where we should camp in the wilderness, and you can be our eyes.'

What a difference a year makes!

It had been almost exactly a year since the Israelites left Egypt and arrived at Mount Sinai. And in that time they had experienced the miracles over Egypt as they left, the Passover, the great crossing at the Red Sea and the making of the covenant at Mount Sinai. There had been the terrible time when they had rebelled against God and almost been destroyed, but had received God's forgiveness. Then they spent some months building the Tabernacle. But now it was time to move on: 'The LORD our God said to us at Horeb, "You have stayed long enough at this mountain"' (Deuteronomy 1:6).

In Numbers 10:29, Moses turns to the family who had first welcomed him to Sinai: the family of Jethro, who was now his father-in-law (see Exodus 18). Moses speaks to Hobab, who was most probably Jethro's son and therefore Moses' brother-in-law, and invites him to accompany him on his journey. Hobab initially declined, but it seems that he eventually agreed because he turns up in Judges chapters 1 and 4. We also read about the Canaanite people of this particular community, later called the Kenites, subsequently being among the Israelites.

So, who was really leading the people at this point? God? Yes: we are told in verse 33 that the Ark of the Covenant, representing the very presence of God, was going before them as they moved, and the cloud of God's presence was seen by day and the pillar of fire by night. God was in charge. What about Moses? In verse 35, he was appointed by God and he had the authority to say when they were going to leave and where they would stop and camp. So what about Hobab? In verse 31, Moses says to him, 'You will be our eyes. You know where the water is, you know where the oasis is; you have the local expertise.'

Moses had God's authority, God's presence and God's guidance, yet he asks for Hobab's eyes. He is confident in God but doesn't despise human expertise and wisdom.

God has given each of us a work to do for him. Perhaps, like the Israelites, he is calling you to begin a new venture. Spend time in God's presence, seek his guidance. But remember, God has strategically placed mature believers in your life so you can learn from their wisdom and experience. Be humble, be ready to learn from others, recognize that 'You are Christ's body – that's who you are! . . . Only as you accept your part of that body does your "part" mean anything' (1 Corinthians 12:27, MSG).

Day 2

Read Numbers 11:1–9
Key verses: Numbers 11:4–6

••

> *4The rabble with them began to crave other food, and again the Israelites started wailing and said, 'If only we had meat to eat! 5We remember the fish we ate in Egypt at no cost – also the cucumbers, melons, leeks, onions and garlic. 6But now we have lost our appetite; we never see anything but this manna!'*

The future was bright.

God's people were on the move. They are led by God, with the presence of God's Spirit, led by Moses and a man with brilliant expertise, Hobab, and with the wonderful promises of good things that God has put ahead of them. Moses mentions twice to Hobab about the good things that God had promised to Israel (10:29, 32).

So chapter 11:1 is a bit of a shock. 'The people complained about their hardships.' The Hebrew word 'hardships' conveys the idea of evil. I'm sure that the narrator is quite deliberately contrasting the double use of 'good' in what Moses said to Hobab with this immediate use of 'evil' in the language and the attitude of the people. They are grumbling, rebellious, and disobedient. The scene in verses 1–3 – the people grumbling, God's anger and judgment, followed by Moses' intervention and the containment of the problem – is replayed throughout the book.

You would be surprised at what the people complained about. What do you think the Israelites would have remembered the most about the years of slavery in Egypt? Just one year before this event they had been an oppressed, exploited minority, being beaten and put to slave labour in Egyptian agriculture and construction projects, doing all the dirty work that the Egyptians didn't want to do. What would they remember? The hard labour, the humiliation, the genocidal murder of the little boys? No. They remember the fish. It was very tasty and it was free. Talk about a selective memory! They reckoned that a healthy diet in slavery was better than a normal diet in freedom. They had been having a miracle a day – manna – but it wasn't good enough and they found it boring. How perverse!

We are not much different from the Israelites. When our circumstances are difficult we are quick to question whether God loves us and is for us. We conveniently ignore all the miracles of grace that God performs each day – simply because life has not turned out how we had hoped or imagined. We quickly forget God's faithfulness to us in the past, the times we have seen his goodness, the answered prayers and the guidance we have received. Today, open your eyes to see God's mercies and remember his acts of kindness to you. Literally, count your blessings; write them down in a list. Praise God for who he is and all he has done.

I will remember the deeds of the LORD;
    yes, I will remember your miracles of long ago.
I will consider all your works
    and meditate on all your mighty deeds.
(Psalm 77:11–12)

Day 3

Read Numbers 11:4–15
Key verses: Numbers 11:12–14

· ·

> ¹²*Did I conceive all these people? Did I give them birth? Why do you tell me to carry them in my arms, as a nurse carries an infant, to the land you promised on oath to their ancestors?* ¹³*Where can I get meat for all these people? They keep wailing to me, 'Give us meat to eat!'* ¹⁴*I cannot carry all these people by myself; the burden is too heavy for me.*

'I'm a failure, get me out of here!'

Moses was a gifted leader. He had all the training, expertise and experience of forty years of government service under Pharaoh, but this massive community protest caused him to doubt his own leadership.

In verse 10 we read: 'The Lord became exceedingly angry, and Moses was troubled.' That's actually a little weak, as the original text says that it was evil in the eyes of Moses.

The narrator is yet again contrasting the good things that were supposed to be happening at the end of chapter 10 with the evil that is happening now. Moses and God are quite rightly angry. Moses has told Hobab that things are going to be good, but now he sees that things have become terribly bad.

It's ironic that in verse 11, Moses accuses God of doing evil to him. The word used in verse 10 is used again here: 'God, why did you do evil to me?' Moses suggests that God should have taken his responsibility as a parent a little more seriously, and not dumped all the chores on to the nanny. He says, 'Lord, I can't take it any more.' This outburst is almost a complete collapse of his self-confidence as a leader. We can look at this positively, and say that at the very least, Moses is not presented here as a James Bond figure. In films, it's amazing how quickly the hero comes up with a solution and always knows exactly what to do. Nor is Moses a management guru, expertly sitting down to diagnose the problem, coming up with creative ideas that will lead to solutions that every-one agrees to and then moves forward. Moses simply collapses. He is face down before the Lord in desperate inadequacy, desperate dependence. There's an absence of self-sufficiency. But I think there's something more serious here. This crisis is causing Moses to doubt not only his own leadership, but God himself.

Feelings of inadequacy and facing criticism are commonplace in Christian ministry. Sadly, opposition does not just come from unbelievers. We also face 'friendly fire' from fellow Christians. Such scenarios can cause us to doubt God when the exact opposite course of action is needed. When you are wounded, cling to Christ more closely, look to him for strength and guidance, trust his word and his promises. Use this time of weakness to deepen your relationship with Christ. Look to him alone for validation and approval.

> Look to the LORD and his strength;
>   seek his face always.
> (Psalm 105:4)

Day 4

Read Numbers 11:16–25
Key verses: Numbers 11:16–17

••

¹⁶The LORD said to Moses: 'Bring me seventy of Israel's elders who are known to you as leaders and officials among the people. Make them come to the tent of meeting, that they may stand there with you. ¹⁷I will come down and speak with you there, and I will take some of the power of the Spirit that is on you and put it on them. They will share the burden of the people with you so that you will not have to carry it alone.

For the first time we hear that Moses is a man of God's Spirit: 'the Spirit that is on you'. What does that mean?

It certainly doesn't mean that Moses had instant solutions to every problem, nor did it give him some super status. Remember that the man who God describes here in verse 17 as having 'the Spirit' is the man in verses 11–15 who wasn't able to cope. We might say, paradoxically, that the fact that he knew he had the Spirit of God reinforced a lack of self-sufficiency. Moses knew that only God could solve the problem, and yet he still felt alone, impotent and inadequate. So God said, 'I'll tell you what I'll do, I'll spread the Spirit around. I'll put the Spirit on seventy more people so they can help you carry the load.'

Back in Exodus 18, the administrative load had already been shared and delegated on the advice of Jethro, so this event is probably talking more about the sharing of spiritual leadership, of widening the circle of those that God had given gifts to, those who were able to administer pastoral wisdom. In verses 24–25 the elders come together before the watching people. They're not appointed by some election; they're summoned here by God's representative and God authenticates them by letting them prophesy. This probably means that they speak some kind of word from God.

Moses was perfectly willing to accept the gifts of the Spirit to and in other people, and that is a sign of his spiritual maturity. Moses teaches us that the Spirit is for sharing. Even though God raises up remarkable individuals within his community of people, of all ages, it is still intended by God that it is a shared leadership, exercised alongside the gifts of others. The New Testament clearly endorses this: the Spirit of God distributed his gifts not just for the one man at the top but to be shared.

God has shared his Spirit with the other believers in your home group, those with whom you serve on rotas, the people you get on with in church – and those you don't! What a sobering thought. Remember Barnabas – even though all the activity in the church outside Jerusalem was very different from his own Jewish upbringing, when he 'saw what the grace of God had done, he was glad' (Acts 11:23). Today, thank God when you see his Spirit working in someone else's life. Find practical ways to encourage that person to continue using their gift for God.

Day 5

Read Numbers 11:24–30
Key verse: Numbers 11:29

· ·

29 But Moses replied, 'Are you jealous for my sake? I wish that all the LORD's people were prophets and that the LORD would put his Spirit on them!'

How do you cope when the unexpected happens?

In the camp, there is an outburst of unscripted, unsupervised charismatic activity. Two men, Eldad and Medad, registered elders, had remained in the camp rather than going out to the tent. Yet the Spirit also rested on them and they began to prophesy. Joshua, son of Nun, Moses' assistant, is outraged and says, 'Moses, my lord, stop them!' (verse 28). Perhaps he was concerned this was a breach of good order, perhaps he thought it was bad manners, perhaps he was afraid of a loss of control, or he thought it was an implied insult to Moses. Often when people are in some position of senior leadership, you find a bunch of acolytes who draw their own authority and status from being servants of the servant of God. Anything that threatens the leader's authority also threatens theirs. Quite possibly Joshua sees the threat to Moses' authority and wonders how it's going to affect him.

In verse 29 we have Moses' reply: 'Are you jealous for my sake?' as if to say, 'It's not a problem to me, so why is it a problem for you?' Moses had no desire for office, status or prestige. If God wanted to share his gifts around, it was no problem for Moses. In fact, he says that he wishes all of God's people were prophets. Perhaps he thought that if they were all prophets, he wouldn't have to be the one sorting out everyone else's problems! Perhaps it was simply that Moses had a deep security in his relationship with God. He had no need to prove anything, and that in itself is a mark of great spiritual maturity.

Our reactions in church and the Christian world, especially when things are unexpected and not quite what we want, can be like Joshua's: 'Stop them; we can't have that going on.' Or our reaction can be like that of Moses. We can be led by the Spirit of God and renounce the attributes the world usually links to strong leadership: self-sufficiency, status, ambition and control.

Check your heart – are you jealous, are you motivated by status and prestige, do you like to be in control? Like Moses, seek security – not in your position or title, but solely in your relationship with God. You are 'in Christ'. You may lose your job, or have to relinquish ministry responsibilities, or your family circumstances may change. You may feel that everything that gave you your identity has been stripped away. But grasp the truth that you are totally complete, accepted, right-eous, alive and secure in Christ. Ask the Holy Spirit to help you renounce worldly leadership traits in favour of pursuing spiritual maturity.

> Do not tie your joy, your sense of well-being, to power in ministry. Your ministry can be taken from you. Tie your joy to the fact you are known and loved by God; tie it to your salvation; tie it to the sublime truth that your name is written in heaven.
> (D. A. Carson, *A Call to Spiritual Reformation*, IVP, 2011, p. 141)

Day 6

Read Numbers 11:18–23, 31–35
Key verses: Numbers 11:33–34

••

> ³³*But while the meat was still between their teeth and before it could be consumed, the anger of the* LORD *burned against the people, and he struck them with a severe plague.* ³⁴*Therefore the place was named Kibroth Hattaavah, because there they buried the people who had craved other food.*

Sometimes physical symptoms mask more serious health issues. In a similar way, God perceives there is more to the people's whining than simply boredom with manna. He sees his people turning away from the whole project of salvation. The Israelites had been crying out in the slavery crisis in Exodus and now they are saying, 'We were better off in Egypt.' They had the living God among them, but had rejected him. 'So,' says God, 'you want meat, I'll give you meat until you're sick of it' (verses 18–20).

The writer tells us in verse 31 that 'a wind went out from the LORD'. In Hebrew that's the word *ruah*, which is exactly the word that is translated as Spirit. The wind or Spirit of God solved the meat crisis by bringing so much quail in on the wind that the people are able to net it and everyone had buckets full. But it leads to serious illness, as we read in verse 33. It sounds like before the actual supply of birds was finished, it went bad. The plague that is described is quite possibly food poisoning. Perhaps they didn't let the meat dry out properly or they didn't salt it properly. The result is more graves in the wilderness. The place, in English, was called, 'Graves of craving'. The people craved meat and it led to their punishment, judgment and suffering.

In the same way, we need to be careful about what lies beneath when there is a culture of complaints and protest in any Christian community. In church, complaints about simple things like food, rotas and the use of money can actually hide a deeper discontent and a deeper failure, especially the failure to understand the deeper plan and purpose of God for us as a church. Sometimes our behaviour can be very thoughtless and faithless and we can be very short in our memories. In spite of all the good things that God has built into the past, and all the good things that he has for the future, we effectively put God's purposes in rewind.

It is frightening to think we can be so consumed by grumbling and dissent that we fail to comprehend God's plan for us. But this danger is real for both the church and individuals. God is working in your difficult circumstances, your grief, and your suffering, whether you can see it or not. Don't get so wrapped up in your complaints that you miss God's comfort, what he is trying to teach you, and how he wants to use you. Today, instead of complaining, will you trust that God, who has worked in your past, is now working in your present?

Day 7

Read Numbers 12:1–9
Key verses: Numbers 12:1–2

....

> [1]*Miriam and Aaron began to talk against Moses because of his Cushite wife, for he had married a Cushite.* [2]*'Has the LORD spoken only through Moses?' they asked. 'Hasn't he also spoken through us?' And the LORD heard this.*

'Who does he think he is?' This was the essence of Aaron and Miriam's complaint against Moses.

At first glance, the conflict seemed to revolve around sibling rivalry. Moses was the younger brother, and you can imagine Aaron and Miriam's jealousy that he was still getting the limelight after all these years. There also seemed to be an ethnic issue. Verse 1 mentions twice that Moses' wife, most likely his second wife, was a Cushite. Cush was an important powerful kingdom just south of biblical Egypt, in what we could now call southern Egypt or part of northern Sudan. His wife would have been a black African. We are not exactly sure why Aaron and Miriam objected to this marriage, but ethnic prejudice and racial hatred seem to have played a part.

However, verse 2 exposes the real source of the conflict. Even though Aaron and Miriam had been appointed by God to their roles (Micah 6:4) – Aaron was a high priest, the head of the whole priesthood in Israel, and Miriam was a prophet (Exodus 15:20) – they were jealous of Moses' position. Moses was the one through whom God was revealing his will, law and word, and Aaron and Miriam questioned his unique relationship to God and his uniqueness in relation to them.

In terms of biblical history and salvation, at this stage of the biblical revelation, Moses certainly did occupy a unique position. It was not because he claimed or wanted it, but because God had chosen him and put him there. It is a familiar tactic among the discontented and disaffected, and insinuates an arrogance about Moses that the narrator is going to tell us is not there. It accuses him of a monopoly that he did not want; it implies that Moses was hogging all the gifts and status, when in fact that was the opposite of what he wanted (Numbers 11). And so Aaron and Miriam protest. Both of them had God-given gifts and responsibilities of their own. But this is a case of spiritual jealousy, discontent and an attack on a brother. It may have looked like a family feud, but there was a profoundly spiritual issue attached.

In John 21, Jesus reinstates Peter after his denial. When Jesus spoke to him about his ministry and how he would die, Peter's first reaction was to look at John, Jesus' beloved disciple, and ask, 'Lord, what about him?' Jesus replied, 'What is that to you? You must follow me' (verse 22). Don't waste time looking around at other people's gifts and how God is using them: what is that to you? Just make sure you are following God and serving him where he has placed you. We won't have to give an account of how anyone else has used their gifts, only how we have used ours (2 Corinthians 5:10).

Day 8

Read Numbers 12:1–9
Key verses: Numbers 12:2–3

....

²*'Has the* L_{ORD} *spoken only through Moses?' they asked. 'Hasn't he also spoken through us?' And the* L_{ORD} *heard this.* ³*(Now Moses was a very humble man, more humble than anyone else on the face of the earth.)*

How do you deal with conflict or attacks on your character?

Notice the contrast between the way that Aaron and Miriam are behaving and the way that Moses reacts. We read that Miriam and Aaron began to talk against Moses. We want to ask where and to whom. To each other? To other people? To other family members? And they asked whom? Themselves? Anyone who would listen? The rest of the Levites? There's a campaign going on, a subtle subversive undermining of Moses. But what does Moses say in response? Nothing. And it seems that the narrator gets embarrassed by this silence. The narrator says that the Lord heard what they were saying but Moses said nothing, and the reason was that Moses was the most humble man on earth. Moses was not a character who got into a dog fight of attack, defence and counter-attack. There was a dignified silence.

One of the things that I've learnt in my limited experience of Christian leadership is that self-defence is rarely, if ever, the right response to being attacked, accused or mis-interpreted. The more you try to defend yourself, the more you dig yourself into a hole, and the more you make the accusations sound as if they are true. Moses' example reminds us that spiritual authority and personal humility are not incompatible but integral to each other; the one is part of the other. Humility is the very essence of a Christian leader amongst God's people.

Humility is not just for Christian leaders but for all disciples of Christ. Today, reflect on Jesus' humility and what it means for you, in your particular situation, to cultivate his mindset.

> In your relationships with one another, have the same mindset as Christ Jesus:
>> Who, being in very nature God,
>>> did not consider equality with God something
>>>> to be used to his own advantage;

rather, he made himself nothing
    by taking the very nature of a servant,
    being made in human likeness.
And being found in appearance as a man,
    he humbled himself
    by becoming obedient to death –
        even death on a cross!
(Philippians 2:5–8)

Can you serve your boss and others at work, helping them to succeed and be happy, even when they are promoted and you are overlooked? Can you work to make others look good without envy filling your heart? Can you minister to the needs of those whom God exalts and men honour when you yourself are neglected? Can you pray for the ministry of others to prosper when it would cast yours in the shadows?
(Donald Whitney, *Spiritual Disciplines for the Christian Life*, NavPress, 1991, p. 122)

Day 9

Read Numbers 12:1–9
Key verse: Numbers 12:7

....

> [7]. . . *my servant Moses;*
> *he is faithful in all my house.*

We all know those words of Jesus that we hope to hear ourselves: 'Well done, good and faithful servant.' Most of us expect to die before we hear them. What happens here is that Moses hears them at this precise point of accusation.

God deals with the quarrel by directly confronting the participants and by calling them together into his presence. He summoned them to the tent of meeting and came down in a pillar of cloud (verses 4–5). We already know that Moses was humble. But now God tells Aaron and Miriam that his servant Moses was faithful (verse 7). Addressing Moses as 'my servant' is in itself a term of high honour combined with humble status. This title of 'my servant' is given to very few people in the Old

Testament. God says this about Caleb, for example, in Numbers 14:24; it's said about David quite regularly, but it's a rare term of honour, speaking about someone who was going to do the will and purpose of God. The fact that Moses is God's servant means that he has access to the whole of his estate. God is saying, 'All of my affairs are entrusted into his hands.' God is saying that he has exercised trust in Moses. He trusted him to confront Pharaoh and to stand firm in all the pressures of the plagues. He trusted Moses to lead this people, he trusted Moses to reveal his law and his name, as Yahweh the God of Israel. And God says, 'My servant Moses has not been a disappointment to me. He has been faithful in every department of my house.' It doesn't mean that Moses didn't make any mistakes, but God is saying that he is a trustworthy house manager.

Can God trust you? Will you remain faithful to him when your prayers seem to go unanswered? Will you keep serving when you can't see the results? Will you work zealously when only God sees your effort? Will you obey him in the small, daily, apparently insignificant moments of life rather than looking to make a grand gesture?

Faithfulness isn't very glamorous. We prefer to applaud success. Today, determine to leave the outcomes with God and concentrate on getting ready for his return by faithfully obeying his Word and doing whatever work he has entrusted to you (Matthew 24:36–37; 25:21).

> It gave me great joy when some believers came and testified about your faithfulness to the truth, telling how you continue to walk in it. I have no greater joy than to hear that my children are walking in the truth.
> (3 John 1:3–4)

Be a loyal servant of Christ so that one day you will hear him say: 'Well done, good and faithful servant!' (Matthew 25:21).

Day 10

Read Numbers 12:1–9
Key verse: Numbers 12:8

....

> [8] *With him I speak face to face,*
> *clearly and not in riddles;*
> *he sees the form of the* LORD.
> *Why then were you not afraid*
> *to speak against my servant Moses?*

We talk of having 'mountain top' encounters with God: times when our experience and appreciation of him is magnified. Perhaps the concept comes from Moses' breath-taking encounters with God, many of which happened on mountains.

God certainly distinguishes between ordinary everyday prophets, to whom he gives messages and dreams, and Moses. With Moses, it's different, as he says: 'With him I speak face to face.' The words in verse 8 convey the idea of speaking mouth to mouth. God says that 'Moses speaks what I say'. There is a direct correlation between the word of Moses and the word of God. God's law and truth and self-revelation at this point in biblical history are coming through this man of God. That is part of the reason for the scriptural authority of Moses. Not only is Moses God's servant, he is also God's friend. Moses has a unique intimacy with God.

Listen to Exodus 33:11–13:

> The LORD would speak to Moses face to face, as one speaks to a friend . . . Moses said to the LORD, 'You have been telling me, "Lead these people," but you have not let me know whom you will send with me. You have said, "I know you by name and you have found favour with me." If you are pleased with me, teach me your ways so I may know you.'

Moses wanted to know God as a friend, and God honoured that request. So in Numbers 12:8, God says that Moses saw 'the form' of the Lord. It doesn't mean that Moses saw God as he was, but that Moses clearly saw some visible expression of the presence of God. Exodus 24, the story of the making of the covenant, tells of some people who saw God. They had a one-off visible experience of the presence of God. The rest of the people, we are told in Deuteronomy 4:12, 15, saw 'no form'; there was only a voice on the day that the Lord spoke through the fire. Moses had a unique experience of the presence of God, so much so that when he went out of the presence of God, his face was shining in such a way that the people were afraid of him. God affirms his approval of his chosen leader Moses, not because of his great power, resourcefulness or managerial skills, but because he was a humble man, a faithful servant, a unique communicator and a true friend of God.

Is it obvious when you have spent time with Jesus? When Moses met with God, his face shone. Your face may not shine but you may be more patient in difficult situations, quicker to forgive, joyful rather than critical, kind rather than bitter. Time with God – studying and praying through his Word (and then obeying it) – is the only way that we become more like Christ. Make these times a priority. Then, like a candle in a cracked clay jar (2 Corinthians 4:7), the life of Christ will shine out through you and draw others to the Saviour.

Day 11

Read Numbers 12:1–9
Key verses: Numbers 12:7–8

. . . .

7. . . my servant Moses;
   he is faithful in all my house.
8 With him I speak face to face,
   clearly and not in riddles;
   he sees the form of the Lord.

Can you imagine being there when Jesus led Cleopas and his friend in a Bible study? Luke 24:27 says, 'And beginning with Moses and all the Prophets, he explained to them what was said in all the Scriptures concerning himself.' Perhaps Jesus mentioned Numbers 12, as he is clearly anticipated in this chapter. Notice how Moses is a portrait of the Lord Jesus Christ:

• Humble

   Moses was a humble man; so was Jesus. That's how he's assessed in Isaiah 53:2–3: 'He had no beauty or majesty to attract us to him, nothing in his appearance that we should desire him. He was despised and rejected by mankind, a man of suffering, and familiar with pain.' Jesus said that 'whoever wants to be first must be slave of all. For even the Son of Man did not come to be served, but to serve, and to give his life as a ransom for many' (Mark 10:44–45).

- Faithful

Just as Moses was faithful, so was Jesus. The writer of the book of Hebrews picks up on this language of Moses and applies it to Jesus in Hebrews 3:6: 'Christ is faithful as the Son over God's house.' In the verse before, he says, '"Moses was faithful as a servant in all God's house," bearing witness to what would be spoken by God in the future.' Jesus knew that he came from the Father and was going to the Father. He was secure in his own Sonship, and so he was able to take the status of a servant and act humbly.

- The unique revelation of God

Moses saw the form of God whereas Jesus was in the form of God; he was a member of the Godhead. As Paul puts it in Philippians 2:6, Jesus was 'in very nature God'. Hebrews 1:1–2 explains that 'God spoke to our ancestors through the prophets at many times and in various ways, but in these last days he has spoken to us by his Son'.

God's words about Moses, although historically true about him, were prophetically true about Jesus, who also bears the mark of God's approval.

Moses' life pointed to Christ, and so should ours. Instead of blending in, our lifestyles should be so distinct and winsome that people start asking, 'Why?' Think: does how you spend your time and money differ greatly from your non-Christian neighbours? Do how you treat work colleagues, what you post on Facebook, the activities in which you encourage your children to be involved, point people towards Christ?

> If I make you light-bearers, you don't think I'm going to hide you under a bucket, do you? I'm putting you on a light stand. Now that I've put you there on a hilltop, on a light stand – shine! Keep open house; be generous with your lives. By opening up to others, you'll prompt people to open up with God, this generous Father in heaven.
>
> (Matthew 5:14–16, MSG)

Day 12

Read Numbers 12:10–16
Key verses: Numbers 12:10–11, 13

....

[10]When the cloud lifted from above the tent, Miriam's skin was leprous – it became as white as snow. Aaron turned towards her and saw that she had a defiling skin disease, [11]and he said to Moses, 'Please, my lord, I ask you not to hold against us the sin we have so foolishly committed . . .' [13]So Moses cried out to the LORD, 'Please, God, heal her!'

We often get angry when our plans are derailed, the computer crashes, or just from waiting in a queue! In stark contrast, God's anger is holy and righteous, and Aaron and Miriam felt the full force of it.

God leaves the tent of meeting, and when the cloud lifts we see Miriam is afflicted with a skin disease. This is not leprosy in its modern form, but probably some form of flaking skin disorder which is described as falling off like snow. Aaron is horrified; in that culture the shame on his sister was also a shame on him. The irony is that Aaron had complained that Moses was usurping the full right to pray and speak to God, but now Aaron doesn't feel it is right to go straight into the presence of God, high priest though he is, so he turns to Moses. And here, for the first time, Moses speaks. This is the only time he speaks in this chapter, and when he does it is to pray for his sister: 'Please, God, heal her!' (verse 13). This is a mark of the likeness of Christ who told us that we should love those who persecute us (Matthew 5:44), and who said, 'Father, forgive them, for they do not know what they are doing' (Luke 23:34). Moses asks God to heal his sister and God does so, after a period of time – a week of disgrace, in which the lesson will be learnt by Miriam and the whole community.

Raymond Brown in his commentary puts it like this: 'Moses learnt the importance of silence and let the Lord do the talking . . . Aaron learnt the value of prayer' – though he was a high priest, he had to learn the power of the prayer of others (his own brother). 'Miriam learnt the generosity of grace' because eventually she was pardoned, cleansed, healed and restored, and 'the people learnt the seriousness of sin', although we have to say that they didn't learn it very well (Raymond Brown, *Numbers*, BST, IVP, 2002, p. 111).

What about us? What do we learn? It depends on whom you identify with in the story. Is the Holy Spirit convicting you that you are behaving like Miriam and Aaron: critical, undermining and jealous, guilty of discontent? If so, let's repent of our ways. Is the Holy Spirit impressing on you the humility of Moses, his integrity in leadership, his reliance on God in difficult days? Is the Holy Spirit urging you to trust God, let him vindicate you and, in due course, exalt you? For God's glory, make it your ambition to be his humble servant.

Day 13

Read Numbers 13:1–33
Key verses: Numbers 13:30–33

....

30 Then Caleb . . . said, 'We should go up and take possession of the land, for we can certainly do it.' 31 But the men who had gone up with him said, 'We can't attack those people; they are stronger than we are.' 32 And they spread among the Israelites a bad report about the land they had explored. They said, 'The land we explored devours those living in it. All the people we saw there are of great size 33 . . . We seemed like grasshoppers in our own eyes, and we looked the same to them.'

They didn't know it yet, but the Israelites were on the brink of arguably the most awful catastrophe in their history up to this point. They arrived at the very southern edges of the land of promise, the oasis that was there at Kadesh, and they decided to send out spies into the land. The spies' initial report is very positive. They tell Moses,

'We went into the land to which you sent us, and it does flow with milk and honey!' (verse 27). They even brought back a big bunch of grapes to prove how fruitful the land was.

But then something happens. In verse 28 the spies' report very suddenly shifts into a grossly exaggerated negative account. Caleb silenced the people before Moses and urged, 'We should go up and take possession of the land, for we can certainly do it.' The other ten spies say, 'Sorry, but we can't.' The ten spies then spread negativity and an inferiority complex among the people: 'We can't attack those people . . . We seemed like grasshoppers in our own eyes' (verses 31, 33). Their account bred fear among the Israelites, which Moses recorded in Deuteronomy 1:28–29: '"Our brothers have made our hearts melt in fear. They say, 'The people are stronger and taller than we are; the cities are large, with walls up to the sky. We even saw the Anakites there.'" Then I said to you, "Do not be terrified; do not be afraid of them."'

As Raymond Brown puts it, the spies 'magnified the problem and then minimised the resources that they had', and their report leads to the people's rebellion (*Numbers*, BST, IVP, 2002, pp. 118–119). 'That night all the members of the community raised their voices and wept aloud. All the Israelites grumbled against Moses and Aaron, and the whole assembly said to them, "If only we had died in Egypt! Or in this wilderness!"' (Numbers 14:1–2).

It is easy to look at the huge problems in our world, the rising opposition to Christianity and the massive task of evangelism, and to feel so fearful and inadequate that we don't actually do anything. But remember that you serve in God's name, with his power and resources. He promises to equip you for all that he calls you to do. Just as he multiplied the five loaves and two fish, he can multiply your efforts and use them for his glory. Today, take heart from God's word to Joshua:

> Have I not commanded you? Be strong and courageous.
> Do not be afraid; do not be discouraged, for the LORD
> your God will be with you wherever you go.
> (Joshua 1:9)

Day 14

Read Numbers 14:1–12
Key verse: Numbers 14:11

....

11 The LORD said to Moses, 'How long will these people treat me with contempt? How long will they refuse to believe in me, in spite of all the signs I have performed among them?'

Listening to a sermon is often a good way to understand a Bible passage. Sometimes the Bible helps us by providing a sermon on its own text; and that's what we get in Deuteronomy 1. In chapters 1–3, Moses remembers what happened in the book of Numbers and preaches to the next generation of Israelites on the basis of this.

Moses' sermon explains what happened in Numbers 13–14: 'But you were unwilling to go up; you rebelled against the command of the LORD your God. You grumbled in your tents and said, "The LORD hates us; so he brought us out of Egypt to deliver us into the hands of the Amorites to destroy us"' (Deuteronomy 1:26–27).

There is this grumbling rebellion against God and a rejection of God's plans, the whole purpose of the redemption. The Israelites had been brought out of Egypt and they wanted to go back. Even worse than that, they attributed false motives to God. They said, 'He only brought us out of slavery because he wanted to kill us here.' They also said, 'The LORD *hates* us' (Deuteronomy 1:27, emphasis added). That's incredible. What they had just experienced was the biggest demonstration of the love and faithfulness of God in the entire Bible, apart from on the cross: the story of the Exodus. It's the Old Testament story of God's redemption, faithfulness, love and power. God has poured his love on these people and they turn around and say, 'Do you know what? God hates us.'

They say, 'We'd rather be dead. We'd rather go back to slavery' (Numbers 14:1–3). What is God's response? He says in verse 11, 'How long will these people treat me with contempt, and how long will they refuse to believe in me?' It's very strong language. It's the kind of language that is used about David's adultery with Bathsheba (2 Samuel 12:14).

This rebellion in the wilderness is not just a rejection of Moses or the leadership; it is a rejection of God himself. The Israelites have a choice to make: they can either please God, and have God be pleased with them, through courage, obedience and faith; or they can oppose and stand against God, and be afraid of those whom God has already defeated (Numbers 14:8–9).

There is a story of a father trying to get his young son to sit down. The father kept asking the boy to sit, but the boy determinedly refused. At last the boy sat down, but he looked his father in the eye and said, 'In my heart I'm standing up!' We may not have rebelled against God as spectacularly as the Israelites, but often our hearts are just as defiant. In the Holy Spirit's power, stop disobedience taking root. Be grateful instead of grumbling; be intentional about remembering God's faithfulness to you. Daily acknowledge and submit to his sovereign will.

Day 15

Read Numbers 14:1–12
Key verses: Numbers 14:10–11

....

[10] But the whole assembly talked about stoning them. Then the glory of the Lord appeared at the tent of meeting to all the Israelites. [11] The Lord said to Moses, 'How long will these people treat me with contempt? How long will they refuse to believe in me, in spite of all the signs I have performed among them?'

You saw how the Lord your God carried you . . . until you reached this place. In spite of this, you did not trust in the Lord your God, who went ahead of you on your journey, in fire by night and in a cloud by day.
(Deuteronomy 1:31–33)

Unbelief was the root cause of the massive rebellion in Numbers 14.

In the same way, unbelief vexed Jesus throughout his ministry. Remember when he was unable to do any good work because of the unbelief among the people. 'You of little faith,' he once said to his disciples (Matthew 8:26). Of course, unbelief can afflict us at any point, even as mature Christian believers, when we're confronted with a future that seems uncertain or when God calls us into some new path of obedience. It is one thing to sing and celebrate all that God has done in the past, but it is quite another to be sure that he'll provide in the future. Unbelief can weave into our hearts and lead to disobedience.

This episode at Kadesh was so serious that it echoes on through the Bible. In Psalm 106:24–27 we read:

> Then they despised the pleasant land;
>   they did not believe his promise.
> They grumbled in their tents
>   and did not obey the LORD.
> So he swore to them with uplifted hand
>   that he would make them fall in the wilderness,
> make their descendants fall among the nations
>   and scatter them throughout the lands.

In the New Testament, Paul mentions this rebellion in 1 Corinthians 10, and so does the writer of Hebrews, in chapter 3:16–19:

Who were they who heard and rebelled? Were they not all those Moses led out of Egypt? And with whom was he angry for forty years? Was it not with those who sinned, whose bodies perished in the wilderness? And to whom did God swear that they would never enter his rest if not to those who disobeyed? So we see that they were not able to enter, because of their unbelief.

Unbelief slithers into our hearts and spreads its poison. Has it stopped you talking about Jesus to colleagues in the office or praying fervently? Has it prompted you to prize financial security or overly protect your children from any hardship and disappointment? Has it stopped you recognizing God's daily blessings? Has unbelief in who God is, what his Word says and what his promises mean for you led you into some disobedience? Today, repent of your unbelief; ask God's help to take him at his word and trust him with your life. Cry out to God like the father in Mark 9:24: 'I do believe; help me overcome my unbelief!' If it would be helpful, pray with a mature Christian about your struggles.

Day 16

Read Numbers 14:10–25
Key verse: Numbers 14:19

· ·

¹⁹In accordance with your great love, forgive the sin of these people, just as you have pardoned them from the time they left Egypt until now.

How do we intercede for people? What should we pray?

God is ready to wipe the Israelites out, but Moses steps into the breach between the people and the wrath of God. He intercedes for them and appeals to God to hold back his anger and bear their sin. He appeals to:

• God's reputation (verses 13–16)

News of the Exodus meant God was already making a name for himself around the region (Exodus 15:14–15). So, Moses argued, 'If you kill the Israelites what will people think? Either they will think that you are incompetent or that you are malicious. They will think you brought the Israelites out of Egypt, planned a future for them but your plan collapsed, or you brought them out to raise their hopes and then dash them. Is this what you want people to say about you?' Moses is concerned about the name and reputation of God.

• God's character (verses 17–19)

After that awful incident of the Golden Calf, Moses asked to see God's glory. God hid Moses in the cleft of the rock and declared his name, Yahweh: 'The LORD, the LORD, the compassionate and gracious God, slow to anger, abounding in love and faithfulness, maintaining love to thousands, and forgiving wickedness, rebellion and sin. Yet he does not leave the guilty unpunished' (Exodus 34:6–7). And Moses says, 'Remember these words, remember your own name?' Then he pleads in Numbers 14:17: 'Now may the Lord's strength be displayed, just as you have declared.' Essentially, Moses is saying, 'I understand your anger. But you have an even greater strength because you are Yahweh. You are the God who has the power to forgive, to carry iniquity and to go on being faithful. That's what makes you the God that you are. That's your real strength. If you want to be really strong, then carry them and forgive them.'

- God's promise (verse 16)

  Moses mentions the land that God promised to Abraham (Exodus 32:12–13). His boldness is astonishing. It's almost as if he is saying, 'How can you contemplate destroying all these people? If you can't keep your promise to Abraham, how can I know you'll keep your promises to me? Is that the kind of God you are?'

- God's covenant (verse 19)

  Moses boldly reminds God of the covenant he made with the Israelites at Mount Sinai (Deuteronomy 9:26). God can't abandon his own people; the ones he brought out of Egypt.

What does Moses teach us about praying? He prays about the things that matter most to God. In Psalm 138:2, David affirms, 'You have exalted above all things your name and your word' (ESV). Moses appeals to the very things that are God's priorities, and pleads with him to act to the glory of his name, to act consistently with his own character and in accordance with his promise. Use this as a framework as you pray for others today.

Day 17

Read Numbers 14:20–38
Key verses: Numbers 14:32–34

....

[32] But you – your bodies will fall in this wilderness. [33] Your children will be shepherds here for forty years, suffering for your unfaithfulness, until the last of your bodies lies in the wilderness. [34] For forty years – one year for each of the forty days you explored the land – you will suffer for your sins and know what it is like to have me against you.

God's forgiveness does not mean we escape the con-sequences of our actions. He responded to Moses' appeal with a declaration of forgiveness (verse 20); the people would not be wiped out instantly. However, this did not mean there would be no punishment. God would continue his plan and purpose through the next gener-ation, but this generation of adults had had their last chance. Their rebellion against God had left him with no alternative but to punish them.

In verses 21–24, we have God's general statement of what is going to happen. Notice the contrast here between what this generation of Israelites had seen and what they would now never see. They had seen all the miracles of God, the Exodus and Sinai, but they would never see the Promised Land because of their contempt for God and their persistent rebellion. God says that this had happened ten times. This could be rhetorical, but the rabbis and Jewish scholars did in fact come up with ten occasions in Exodus and Numbers which were instances of grumbling, murmuring and rebellion: at the Red Sea (Exodus 14), Marah (Exodus 15), the Desert of Sinai (three times in Exodus 16), Rephidim (Exodus 17), Sinai (Exodus 32), Taberah (Numbers 11:1–3), Kibroth (Numbers 11:4–34) and here at Kadesh (Numbers 13–14).

In verses 26–35, God goes a little further, filling in the specific details of the punishment. The point of the contrast here is not between what the Israelites had *seen* and would never see, but between what the Israelites had *said* and how God takes them at their word. Earlier in the chapter they'd said, 'We wish we'd died in Egypt or here. We'd rather be dead than go on.' God says, 'Very well, have it your way' (verse 28). They'd also said that their children would be captured as plunder (verse 3) but God says, 'No, they won't. They will be shepherded here in the wilderness until all of the parents die off and then they will go in and enjoy the land that you can't have' (verse 33). This is a sobering tale of a people unrepentantly resistant to God's plan for them, who constantly reject his grace, provision, purposes and love.

For the Israelites, the punishment for sin was death. Likewise, our sin warrants death, but thank God that Jesus died in our place; he became our substitute. He appeased God's wrath and he paid the penalty our sin deserved so that we don't have to (Romans 6:23). We now enjoy a relationship with God where God himself, the Holy Spirit, helps us live to please him. Praise God for this glorious gospel of grace.

Day 18

Read Numbers 14:26–45
Key verses: Numbers 14:42–43

....

⁴²Do not go up, because the Lᴏʀᴅ is not with you. You will be defeated by your enemies, ⁴³for the Amalekites and the Canaanites will face you there. Because you have turned away from the Lᴏʀᴅ, he will not be with you and you will fall by the sword.

Is there a future for God's people?

After God announces his punishment, the people respond with great mourning and a futile effort at belated obedience. They try to enter Canaan but they get beaten back, because the Lord isn't with them. That generation is finished, but God hadn't finished with his plans or the salvation, ultimately, of the world through them. The next thirty-eight years that they were to spend in the wilderness were not to be wasted time. In fact, there are two ways that we can look at this narrative of Kadesh and the following story of the later generation in the wilderness.

We can look at it through the eyes of Psalm 95:10–11, where God declares his anger. We can also look at how Moses speaks to the Israelites in Deuteronomy 8:2–3 about the same event:

> Remember how the Lord your God led you all the way in the wilderness . . . to humble and test you in order to know . . . whether or not you would keep his commands. He humbled you, causing you to hunger and then feeding you with manna . . . to teach you that man does not live on bread alone but on every word that comes from the mouth of the Lord.

God gave them bread to teach them that there were things more important than bread: the word and promise of God. 'Know then in your heart that as a man disciplines his son, so the Lord your God disciplines you' (Deuteronomy 8:5). At one level, the years in the desert were a huge waste of time, the result of sin and rebellion, yet God turns it into a learning experience, an act of parental discipline, and an opportunity for grace and obedience.

It's interesting that in 1 Corinthians 10:11, Paul says that these things were written as *warnings* for us. But in Romans 15:4, he says that these things were written to *teach* us, 'so that through the endurance taught in the Scriptures and the encouragement they provide we might have hope'. Where is the encouragement in this passage? It is that God turns the wilderness into a time of fresh opportunity to love, trust and obey him.

You may feel like you are living in the wilderness because of some past act of rebellion, disobedience to God or folly. Your life feels blighted; you feel you've missed plan A and you're now in plan B. Don't fall for that nonsense! God is patient. You may be in a time of discipline as the Israelites were in the wilderness, but it's not your final destination or where he wants you to stay. Redeem the time, and return to God in love and obedience. When you do, he will respond with grace and blessing.

Day 19

Read Numbers 16:1–15
Key verses: Numbers 16:1–3

....

*¹Korah . . . and certain Reubenites – Dathan and Abiram, sons of Eliab, and On son of Peleth – became insolent ². . . With them were 250 Israelite men . . . ³They came as a group to oppose Moses and Aaron and said to them, 'You have gone too far! The whole community is holy, every one of them, and the L*ORD *is with them.'*

It only takes a few complaints to trigger widespread rebellion. Here, two groups are involved in this challenge against Moses, but it started out as independent grumbles involving three or four individuals. There is Korah of the Levites, and Dathan and Abiram of the Reubenites.

Korah and the Levites were discontented over their status (verse 3). They appeal to very plausible scriptural truth, that the whole community of God's people is holy. This is true. Israel as a whole was intended to be God's holy people (Exodus 19:6). The narrator intends a flashback to Numbers 15:37–41, where God commanded the Israelites to sew tassels on to the hems of their garments so that, even on their clothing, everyone in the community was reminded of their holiness. So, asks Korah, 'Why are Aaron and the priests regarded as more holy than anyone else? What's so special about them?' This is jealousy expressing itself as an issue of equality.

The second theological theme that they appeal to is that the Lord is among all the people (verse 3). This is again true. The Tabernacle itself was a symbol of the presence of God in the midst of the whole people (Exodus 29:45). Korah argues, 'God dwells among all of us, so what gives Aaron and the priests special right of access into the presence of God?' Again, it's a demand of equality, based on spiritual truth. But they're ignoring the particular calling and symbolic function that God had laid on Aaron and the priests in the tribe of Levi.

What were they really after? In verses 9–11, Moses exposes their real motives: they were dissatisfied with the roles that God had given them. The Levites had a tribal responsibility to carry and look after the Tabernacle. But within the tribe of Levi, Aaron and his family had a specific priestly responsibility. It was they alone whom God had commissioned to come to the altar to do the manipulation of the blood for the sacrifices: to speak the words of atonement and blessing, to enter once a year into the holy presence of God and many other duties. The Levites (through Korah) were discontented with what God had given them and jealous of what God had given to others (Aaron and sons); they had ambitions for a higher level of authority, and all the perks that went with it.

Do you desire the status, prestige or label of 'leader', in whatever ministry context you serve, more than actually being a godly servant-leader? Don't give selfish ambition room to grow. Instead, make much of Christ. Pray that you would be a leader like King David, who:

shepherded [the Israelites] with integrity of heart;
    with skilful hands he led them.
(Psalm 78:72)

Day 20

Read Numbers 16:1–15
Key verse: Numbers 16:3

∙∙∙

³*They came as a group to oppose Moses and Aaron and said to them, 'You have gone too far! The whole community is holy, every one of them, and the Lᴏʀᴅ is with them. Why then do you set yourselves above the Lᴏʀᴅ's assembly?'*

Resisting authority, of any sort, is quite common today, but it's not a new phenomenon. It was at the heart of Dathan and Abiram's objection to Moses. It's probable that the second half of verse 3 is Dathan and Abiram's complaint: 'Why then do you set yourselves above the Lᴏʀᴅ's assembly?' In other words, 'Who gave you the right to be in charge?' There is a tension between the equality of all God's people and the God-appointed role and necessity that there should be leaders. It's a tension that God's people have never seemed to get quite right.

But there's much more than a theological conflict. Moses summons these people in to try to sort this out, but they refuse to meet him (verses 12, 14). In verses 13–14, there are perverse and defiant accusations against Moses: 'Isn't it enough that you have brought us up out of a land flowing with milk and honey to kill us in the wilderness? And now you also want to lord it over us!' They attribute to Moses the same evil intention that they had attributed to God: 'You brought us up to kill us in the desert. That's what you want, isn't it, Moses? You want us all dead. You want to lord it over us.'

Why were these people not going into a land of milk and honey? It wasn't because Moses didn't lead them there; it was the people who refused. They held God's leaders in contempt and they refused to accept the leadership that God had appointed. Here we see the perversity of the people who attribute their own failure to the leadership of the people.

This account is not a licence for self-appointed tyrannical leaders to demand unquestioning submission. Neither is it a prohibition against ever questioning our leaders. Certainly we need to be careful about putting ourselves in opposition against those who are in leadership over God's people. Any challenges need to presented with gentleness and respect, speaking the truth in love (Ephesians 4:15). How do you treat your church leaders? Is there anything you could do to show your support and appreciation of them?

> Remember your leaders, who spoke the word of God to you. Consider the outcome of their way of life and imitate their faith . . . Have confidence in your leaders and submit to their authority, because they keep watch over you as those who must give an account. Do this so that their work will be a joy, not a burden, for that would be of no benefit to you.
> (Hebrews 13:7, 17)

If you are a church leader, meditate on Paul's charge to the Ephesian elders:

> Keep watch over yourselves and all the flock of which the Holy Spirit has made you overseers. Be shepherds of the church of God, which he bought with his own blood.
> (Acts 20:28)

Day 21

Read Numbers 16:1–15
Key verse: Numbers 16:15

∙∙

¹⁵ Then Moses became very angry and said to the LORD, 'Do not accept their offering. I have not taken so much as a donkey from them, nor have I wronged any of them.'

Being a leader among God's people is often like being blotting paper. Blotting paper mops up spilt ink. Sometimes that's what leaders have to do: absorb the mess and clean it up. But on this occasion, Moses became very angry. We're told in Numbers 12:3 that Moses was a very humble man. So what sparked this reaction?

I think that it was the last phrase of verse 13 where they accuse him of 'want[ing] to lord it over us'. The first time that Moses had heard these words was forty years before in Egypt, when he had tried to help his own people by killing an Egyptian (Exodus 2:14). That had led to forty years in the wilderness for Moses. Now these people have been so rebellious that Moses is going to have to spend another forty years in the wilderness with them. And the tune still hasn't changed. They still accuse him of wanting to 'lord it over' them. Moses knew deep in his heart that he would rather be anywhere else than in this position of leadership, so this was an unjust accusation against him. And he becomes very angry, and protests to God against this accusation, which he feels is so unforgivably unfair. He says, 'I have not taken so much as a donkey from them' – a typical Jewish way of declaring your own innocence. He's saying, 'Lord, I've done nothing to deserve this kind of accusation. Don't forgive them, don't accept their offering.'

This is the same man who, in Exodus 32:32, asked God to blot his name out of the Book of Life rather than destroy anyone, the same man who had pleaded with God to forgive the people for the rebellion (Numbers 14:13–19). But Moses is a man of flesh and blood, and he explodes with anger.

Think of Abraham, David, Peter, Paul – any leader from the Bible – and you will find an individual who has failed, usually more than once. Every believer is familiar with failure, with times when we have too easily given into sin rather than live up to our holy calling as God's children. But with God, failure isn't final. Repentance offers us a fresh opportunity to live for him in love and obedience. Today, will you ask for and accept God's forgiveness? Will you rely on the Holy Spirit to learn from past failure and move forward in his strength?

> Most Bible characters met with failure and survived. Even when the failure was immense, those who found leadership again refused to lie in the dust and bemoan their tragedy. In fact, their failure and repentance led to a greater conception of God's grace. They came to know the God of the second chance, and sometimes the third and fourth.
>
> (Oswald Sanders, *Spiritual Leadership*, Moody Publishers, 1967, p. 134)

Day 22

Read Numbers 16:16–40
Key verses: Numbers 16:33, 35

. . . .

33 They [those associated with Korah] went down alive into the realm of the dead, with everything they owned; the earth closed over them, and they perished and were gone from the community . . . 35 And fire came out from the LORD and consumed the 250 men who were offering the incense.

Like in the best of stories, the suspense builds as the narrator interweaves what happens to Korah and the Levite supporters with what happens with Dathan, Abiram and his Reubenite supporters. First, look at God's verdict on Korah and the Levites. They claimed to be as holy as the priests, so Moses jumps to the defence of his brother Aaron and proposes a test (verses 16–19). He says, 'Bring your censers. Light your fires, burn the incense and let's see if God accepts you.' What happens? Verse 35: 'fire came out from the LORD and consumed the 250 men who were offering the incense.' The verdict is clear, verse 40: 'This was to remind the Israelites that no one except a descendant of Aaron should come to burn incense before the Lord, or he would become like Korah and his followers.'

What happens to Dathan and Abiram? God tells Moses to warn the Israelites to separate themselves from these defiant rebels. Verses 28–30 are important to the way in which Moses describes the actual conflict: 'This is how you will know that the Lord has sent me to do all these things and that it was not my idea.' Moses passes the decision on to God, saying, 'Let God show the truth.' The truth is twofold: positively, that 'God sent me' and negatively, 'This is not my idea. This has all come from the will, purpose and plan of God.' Moses' authority and plan of action have all come from God and he wants the people to know who they are really opposing: they are showing contempt for God, not just him.

Judgment was immediate and extraordinary (verses 31–34): 'the ground under them split apart and the earth opened its mouth and swallowed them and their households . . . together with their possessions.' Part of the horror of the story is that the God who created the earth for our blessing and enjoyment uses it as the ground for his awesome judgment. In both cases, God acted to defend what he had established: Aaron's unique priesthood and Moses' unique authority. Neither of them vindicated themselves; God made his verdict unmistakable.

God's judgment is real and serious. Despite what it looks like in the world around us, sin will not go unpunished. Jesus paid the penalty for sin when he died on the cross so that those who belong to him will meet him as Saviour rather than Judge (Hebrews 9:26–27). But those who reject Christ, who continue in unrepentant, defiant rebellion, will face the full force of God's wrath (Romans 2:5). Pray for unbelieving family and friends to accept the gospel and turn to Christ while there is still time to repent.

Today, if you hear his voice,
    do not harden your hearts.
(Hebrews 3:7–8)

Day 23

Read Numbers 16:20–45
Key verse: Numbers 16:22

....

22 But Moses and Aaron fell face down and cried out, 'O God, the God who gives breath to all living things, will you be angry with the entire assembly when only one man sins?'

We can pray sitting, standing or kneeling; we can pray anywhere and at any time. There is no posture that makes our prayers more acceptable to God. However, our posture does reveal something about our attitude to prayer and what we are praying about.

Three times in this one chapter, Moses falls on his face (verses 4, 22, 45). Twice in this chapter Moses specifically intercedes with God; he falls on his face to plead for mercy and seek to provide atonement. On the two occasions, in verses 21 and 45, God speaks identical words: 'Get away from this assembly so I can put an end to them at once.' In verse 22, Moses acts in response to that when he appeals to the justice of God, just as Abraham did when he interceded for Sodom and Gomorrah (Genesis 18:16–33). Moses intercedes with God on the basis of his known character. He's the God of all people, the God of justice, and so Moses says, 'You must judge, but let your judgment be discriminating on those who are truly the offenders.' Moses prayed that God would act appropriately and not punish the whole of his people for the offence of a few.

In verse 41 we read, 'The next day the whole Israelite community grumbled against Moses and Aaron. "You have killed the LORD's people," they said.' Neither aspect of this accusation was true. It wasn't Moses or Aaron who had killed anyone; it was God, who had acted without human agency. And Korah, Dathan and Abiram, by their actions, had ceased to be part of the Lord's people. They had set themselves up as enemies of God. The tragedy in the Old Testament is that the whole people of Israel would discover what it would mean to have God as their enemy and to be treated no longer as his people.

Notice that there is an awesome and fearless escalation of sin. This started with Korah, then it became a gang of four (with Dathan, Abiram and On) and then all 250 of the leaders. A day later it had become the whole of Israel. There is something frightfully infectious about sin.

Many Christians ask, 'What is Jesus doing now?' One thing we can be certain of: he is interceding for us before God. In this sense, Moses prefigured Christ. Imagine, God himself is praying to God on your behalf! Jesus is praying for your perseverance in the faith, he is refuting charges that Satan brings against you and he is representing you before God. Today, as you face difficulties and challenges, remember that Jesus is praying for you.

> Who will bring any charge against those whom God has chosen? It is God who justifies. Who then is the one who condemns? No one. Christ Jesus who died – more than that, who was raised to life – is at the right hand of God and is also interceding for us.
> (Romans 8:33–34)

Day 24

Read Numbers 16:42–50
Key verses: Numbers 16:46–47

∙∙∙

46 Then Moses said to Aaron, 'Take your censer and put incense in it, along with burning coals from the altar, and hurry to the assembly to make atonement for them. Wrath has come out from the LORD; the plague has started.' 47 So Aaron did as Moses said, and ran into the midst of the assembly. The plague had already started among the people, but Aaron offered the incense and made atonement for them.

There is a false dichotomy that says the Old Testament God is the God of wrath and the God of the New Testament is a God of mercy. The wrath and mercy of God are in both Testaments. This story gives us a glimpse of that wrath and mercy meeting.

In verse 45 God threatens total destruction, and in verse 46 Moses acts, no longer only in prayer. Moses sent Aaron, Israel's great High Priest, the one whom God himself had appointed to stand in the gap and to atone for his people. Aaron physically puts himself between the people of God and the wrath of God. The language of atonement is spoken of twice (verses 46, 47). It's the same word that is used in the context of the sacrifices mentioned in Leviticus, when it speaks of both the cleansing away of sin and the averting of the wrath of God from the sinner. Aaron, here as elsewhere, is a symbolic portrait of the work of the Lord Jesus Christ.

The emphasis in the concluding verse is that only Aaron can function as the High Priest, and that's confirmed in chapter 17 through the budding of Aaron's staff, proving that he is the one whom God has chosen to stand as his atoning agent. At this point in Israel's history, Aaron was the only one who could make atonement for all Israel, and we know from the Scriptures that Jesus is the only one appointed by God who can make atonement for all the world and all humanity. He is the 'Lamb of God, who takes away the sin of the world' (John 1:29). Let's give thanks to God for his grace.

Aaron, the High Priest, atoned for the sins of the Israelites, but he points forward to our Great High Priest. Whereas Aaron and his descendants had to offer sacrifices for their own sin as well as the sins of the people and keep repeating the ritual – because the blood of bulls and goats never effectively and finally dealt with sin – Jesus was the once-and-for-all atoning sacrifice (Hebrews 7:23–28). His sacrifice on the cross cleanses us from sin and satisfies God's wrath.

> So then, since we have a great High Priest who has entered heaven, Jesus the Son of God, let us hold firmly to what we believe. This High Priest of ours understands our weaknesses, for he faced all of the same testings we do, yet he did not sin. So let us come boldly to the throne of our gracious God. There we will receive his mercy, and we will find grace to help us when we need it most.
> (Hebrews 4:14–16, NLT)

Day 25

Read Numbers 22:1–20
Key verses: Numbers 22:5–6

∙∙∙

⁵Balak said: 'A people has come out of Egypt; they cover the face of the land and have settled next to me. ⁶Now come and put a curse on these people, because they are too powerful for me. Perhaps then I will be able to defeat them and drive them out of the land. For I know that whoever you bless is blessed, and whoever you curse is cursed.'

Fear was spreading. This moving horde of Israelites that had come out of the wilderness had defeated the Amorites, and Moab, the kingdom where the Israelites were camping at this point, was scared that it would suffer the same fate. Of course, only the Israelites knew that God had told them not to attack Moab or take any of their land (Deuteronomy 2:9). The king of Moab, Balak, was certain he couldn't defeat the Israelites in battle, so he decides to turn to sorcery and sends for the best magician around, Balaam, the son of Beor. It took about three weeks for the king's messengers to reach Balaam and three weeks to get back, and they did the journey twice, so it took Balak more than three months to get hold of Balaam.

In verses 7–20, Balak's messengers arrive and bring their fee. It's late, so they stay the night. Balaam consulted God, who gave him two clear instructions: 'Do not go with them' and 'You must not put a curse on those people, because they are blessed' (verse 12). The next morning Balaam gives an answer to the embassy from Moab, but he only gives half of God's answer. He says, 'God has told me not to come' (verse 13). He doesn't tell them that God has told him not to curse them. So the men go back to Balak and report the answer (verse 14). Balak doesn't know Balaam has been told not to curse them, and assumes it's just a question of a higher fee. So he sends a higher offer. Balaam gives a remarkable reply: 'Even if Balak gave me all the silver and gold in his palace, I could not do anything great or small to go beyond the command of the LORD my God' (verse 18). Is this pagan seer genuinely talking like this? Or is this a safety clause in the contract that he hopes he can waive later on? In the night, God tells Balaam to go to Balak, 'but do only what I tell you' (verse 20).

Balaam is a pagan seer and yet God uses him. God does not confine himself to using the godly and upright to fulfil his plans and purposes. He used Pharaoh to release the Israelites from Egypt (Exodus 12:31), the Babylonians to punish the Israelites (Habakkuk 1:5–6) and Cyrus the pagan king of Persia to free the Jews from Babylonian captivity (Isaiah 44:28). Even today, although unbelievers do not recognize it, God is achieving his purpose through them. Today we can trust in God's sovereignty, knowing that his will is being accomplished.

Day 26

Read Numbers 22:21–40
Key verse: Numbers 22:31

• •

> [31] *Then the L*ORD *opened Balaam's eyes, and he saw the angel of the L*ORD *standing in the road with his sword drawn. So he bowed low and fell face down.*

What makes God angry?

In verse 22, Balaam is doing what God told him to do and setting off for Moab, yet God is very angry. Why? The only explanation is that God perceived that Balaam's intention in going was wrong. Balaam makes his living by manipulating gods and spirits to do whatever purpose he gets paid for. So he's probably expecting that when the time comes, he'll be able to do the same again and collect the biggest fee from the richest customer he has ever had: the king of Moab.

God sends his angel to confront Balaam, and the comedy with the donkey begins. Three times in the story the angel of God, with a drawn sword, stands in front of Balaam and the donkey. Balaam doesn't see the angel but the donkey does, and three times the donkey tries to avoid taking action. In verses 28–30, God even opens the mouth of the donkey.

The narrator piles irony upon irony in this part of the story. Think of the number of contrasts happening here. The man on the donkey is called a seer, but he can't see what's in front of his eyes; the donkey sees what the seer can't. Balaam gets paid to be eloquent: this dumb animal gets beaten until he's the one who talks first. The donkey turns aside from the way his master wants him to go, as Balaam is intent on doing. Balaam gets angry with the donkey; God is angry with Balaam. Balaam says he would kill the donkey if only he had a sword in his hand instead of a stick; the angel, who does have a sword in his hand, says that it is only the donkey that saves Balaam's life. Balaam is trying to get the donkey to do what Balak is trying to get Balaam to do – what he wants. Balaam tries beating; Balak tries bribing. The results are equally ineffective. Balak, the king of Moab, is blind to the reality of the God that he's dealing with: so is Balaam until God opens his eyes. The donkey sees the angel of God and then God opens its mouth. Eventually Balaam, God's other ass in the story, is led to see the revelation of God and compelled to speak God's words.

Are your eyes open to what God is doing? Like Balaam the seer and the Pharisees in the New Testament, sometimes it is the very people who claim to have spiritual sight who are the most blind. We need God to open our eyes, not only for the first time at conversion, but daily so that we are alive to who he is, what he says in his Word and what he's doing in the world. Ask God to open your eyes and then, like Balaam, fall on your face in worship and do whatever he tells you to do.

Day 27

Read Numbers 23:1–12
Key verse: Numbers 23:8

....

> [8] *How can I curse*
> *those whom God has not cursed?*
> *How can I denounce*
> *those whom the LORD has not denounced?*

If we go out to eat at a high-class restaurant or buy an expensive gift, we expect to get our money's worth. Balak was definitely not getting what he paid for, because Balaam was unable to curse the Israelites. Why? Because these were the people whom God had promised in his blessing with Abraham:

> I will bless those who bless you,
> and whoever curses you I will curse.
> (Genesis 12:3)

Old Testament Israel was protected by this promise.

There is a further hint at this in Numbers 23:10 as Balaam says, 'Who can count the dust of Jacob or number even a fourth of Israel?' This reference to the dust of the people is clearly an echo of Genesis 13:16. God promised Abraham that his descendants would be as numerous as the sand on the shore, the dust on the earth and the stars in the sky. Here are a people who stand under the protection of God because of what God has promised to Abraham.

Israel in the Old Testament is unique. In verse 9 Balaam says: 'From the rocky peaks I see them, from the heights I view them. I see a people who live apart and do not consider themselves one of the nations.' This doesn't mean that the Israelites are hermits or that there's exclusiveness here. God is saying that he has done things to and for Israel that he has done for no other nation. This is affirmed in Deuteronomy and elsewhere.

Why are these people unique? Why is God doing this? We return to Abraham again; it is for the sake of the nations, and ultimately for the blessing of the nations. This is God's mission, which is why he makes these promises and provides this protection. Balaam is so impressed with this first oracle that he wishes he could share it: 'Let me die the death of the righteous, and may my final end be like theirs!' (verse 10). Tragically, he did not (Numbers 31:8).

As believers, we sin and fail God spectacularly (see Numbers 25 for Israel's failure). But, just like the Israelites, our sin does not exclude us from God's family; we're still his people, still in a covenant relationship with him. Our sin does not cancel out God's great blessings and promises. Even as a church, though we are a community of failed sinners, we are still a community of God's people who trust in his protection, vision and promise. Today, praise God that we live under his overarching protection, promises and blessings. Though we often waver in our commitment and obedience to him, he never wavers in his commitment to us. While we are often faithless, he is always faithful. He is the great Promise-keeper. We can trust who he is and everything he says.

Day 28

Read Numbers 23:13–26
Key verses: Numbers 23:21–22

....

> ²¹ No misfortune is seen in Jacob,
>   no misery observed in Israel.
> The Lᴏʀᴅ their God is with them;
>   the shout of the King is among them.
> ²² God brought them out of Egypt;
>   they have the strength of a wild ox.

Sometimes we lose sight of the awesome holiness and 'otherness' of God, and we treat him as if he were our puppet: someone we can control and manipulate. We twist his words and take them out of context until he says what we want him to say. Before the second oracle, Barak tried to manipulate this God, whoever he is, into a change of mind. He found out, as we all do, that this is not possible: 'God is not human, that he should lie, not a human being, that he should change his mind' (verse 19). In verses 18–24 Balaam utters his oracle. Again there are no curses, only blessing: 'I have received a command to bless; he has blessed, and I cannot change it' (verse 20).

Verse 21 is a little puzzling in its first half: 'No misfortune is seen in Jacob, no misery observed in Israel.' Perhaps it means that in spite of all the problems, Israel will survive. Or perhaps the NIV is right in the footnote translation that says '[God] has not looked on Jacob's offences or the wrongs found.' The sins are there, but God will ultimately cleanse and forgive them.

The real point of this second oracle comes in the second half of verse 21 and verse 22: God has brought these people up out of Egypt and now he's among them as the victorious king. Balaam says, 'There is no divination against Jacob, no evil omens against Israel. It will now be said of Jacob and of Israel, "See what God has done!"' (verse 23). The salvation, the redemption and all that God has done for these people is God's work, and Balaam says, 'I can't stand against them; it's the work of God.' God's people are secure: God is their King (verse 21), their Redeemer (verse 22) and their Protector (verse 23).

God is in the rescue business. The salvation and redemption of the Israelites in the Exodus was all God's work. And our salvation and redemption, won by Christ on the cross, is all God's work too; we can't take any credit (Colossians 1:13–14). Now, God lives not just *among* us as a victorious King, as he did with the Israelites, but *in* us. Paul explains the great privilege we have:

> Christ in you, the hope of glory.
> (Colossians 1:27)

Today, thank God for his presence in your life – submit to him as King, worship him for the price he paid to be your Redeemer, rest secure knowing that he is your Protector. Pray that the Holy Spirit would help you to say 'no' to sin and 'yes' to righteousness, so that Christ would feel more and more at home in your heart.

Day 29

Read Numbers 23:27 – 24:14
Key verses: Numbers 24:5–7

∙∙∙

> [5] *How beautiful are your tents, Jacob,*
> *your dwelling-places, Israel!*
> [6] *Like valleys they spread out,*
> *like gardens beside a river,*
> *like aloes planted by the LORD,*
> *like cedars beside the waters.*
> [7] *Water will flow from their buckets;*
> *their seed will have abundant water.*

God is not limited in those through whom he can speak. He has been speaking through Balaam all along, but the narrator of Numbers makes very clear that in this third oracle, Balaam is speaking by the Spirit of the living God (verse 2). The last time we saw the Spirit of God was in chapter 11, when the Spirit was on Moses and the seventy elders. Here the Spirit comes on a pagan seer.

At this point, Balaam appears to realize what he's up against: 'when Balaam saw that it pleased the Lord to bless Israel, he did not resort to divination as at other times, but turned his face towards the wilderness. When Balaam looked out and saw Israel encamped tribe by tribe, the Spirit of God came on him and he spoke his message' (verses 1–3).

The first oracle was about the past: the promise of God to Abraham. The second oracle was closer to the present because it refers to the Exodus and the Sinai experience, and how God is in the midst of these people. This third oracle (and the fourth) looks much more into the future, and the blessing and the peace that is going to come to this people. God's people will be secure because of his abundant provision for them. Verses 5–7 are a beautiful picture of that provision. The word for 'beautiful' is the same word that we heard in Numbers 10:29 when Moses said to Hobab, 'the Lord has promised *good* things to Israel' (emphasis added). Even Balaam can see this good as he looks to the people. This is a picture of peace, prosperity and abundance, and at one level it's poetic: it points towards an ideal picture of Canaan to which Israel went and centuries later was going to lose because of its sin.

This picture of the land points us forward to the Lord Jesus Christ. In the New Testament, the land of Israel is no longer significant as territory; instead it is taken up into what we now have in Christ. The writer to the Hebrews explains that we don't belong to an earthly city, but are citizens of God's country and part of his family. The Old Testament teaching on the land also points further into the future, to God dwelling with his people in the new heavens and new earth.

You are rich! You may look around at the material wealth of others and shake your head, but as believers in Christ, we enjoy abundant provision. 'In Christ' we know out-of-the-world peace that money can't buy; we experience our Heavenly Father's mercy, grace and kindness daily; and we look forward to a breath-taking inheritance, for ever with the Lord in the new heaven and new earth. Today, prove the sufficiency of Christ; rely on him alone to satisfy your deepest needs.

Day 30

Read Numbers 24:14–25

Key verse: Numbers 24:17

• •

¹⁷*I see him, but not now;*
I behold him, but not near.
A star will come out of Jacob;
a sceptre will rise out of Israel.
He will crush the foreheads of Moab,
the skulls of all the people of Sheth.

How do you respond when your plans are frustrated?
Balak was extremely angry and reprimanded Balaam: 'I
summoned you to curse my enemies, but you have
blessed them these three times. Now leave at once and
go home! I said I would reward you handsomely, but the
LORD has kept you from being rewarded' (verses 10–11).
Balaam replies, 'I'm sorry. I said I wasn't going to be able
to bring anything but blessings. Now I'm going to warn
you about what you and the Moabites can expect in the
future.'

This fourth oracle runs from verses 15 to 25 and is God's messianic promise. The key text is verse 17. In Old Testament history, as these oracles were recorded and eventually passed on, this would have been seen as referring to King David, who did subdue Moab and the other kingdoms. A sceptre, a king, arose in Israel who did exactly what Balaam had said. But as we look at this verse and the great sweep of biblical history, it also points forward to David's greater Son, the one who came as the Messiah King, to Jesus who brought with him the reign of God, not just over Israel but ultimately over all the nations of the world.

These four oracles have taken us from the distant past to the distant future, from Abraham to the Messiah. In this inspired poetry of a soothsayer, God, through his Spirit, spreads before us his whole counsel. First we have God's promise to Abraham and his blessing on Israel for the sake of the whole world. Second, Balaam speaks about God's redemption of his people, the Exodus which prefigures the cross, as the New Testament teaches us. Having redeemed his people, God remains present among them. Third, Balaam speaks about God's provision for his people, in both this world and the world to come. Fourth, he mentions God's messianic reign, the one who would come in the form of David but ultimately in the servant messianic kingship of Christ. What a declaration of the ultimate security of God's people!

You may be serving God in a tough situation, or perhaps you are fearful for your church, where the Christians are vulnerable and young in the faith. God's words of promise and protection are for you. They do not mean you will not suffer persecution, danger or death, but they do mean that the Lord knows those who are his, and he will protect you for eternity. Paul's words leave us in no doubt that we have a sure foundation for our faith, hope and future:

> For I am convinced that neither death nor life, neither angels nor demons, neither the present nor the future, nor any powers, neither height nor depth, nor anything else in all creation, will be able to separate us from the love of God that is in Christ Jesus our Lord.
> (Romans 8:38–39)

For further study

If you would like to do further study on Numbers, the following books may be useful.

- Raymond Brown, *The Message of Romans* (Bible Speaks Today) (IVP, 2002)

- Dennis Cole, *Numbers* (New American Commentary) (Broadman & Holman, 2000)

- Iain Duguid, *Numbers* (Preaching the Word) (Crossway, 2006)

- Roy Gane, *Leviticus, Numbers* (NIV Application Commentary) (Zondervan, 2004)

- Gordon Wenham, *Numbers* (Tyndale Old Testament Commentary) (IVP, 2008)

KESWICK MINISTRIES

Our purpose
Keswick Ministries is committed to the spiritual renewal of God's people for his mission in the world.

God's purpose is to bring his blessing to all the nations of the world. That promise of blessing, which touches every aspect of human life, is ultimately fulfilled through the life, death, resurrection, ascension and future return of Christ. All of the people of God are called to participate in his missionary purposes, wherever he may place them. The central vision of Keswick Ministries is to see the people of God equipped, encouraged and refreshed to fulfil that calling, directed and guided by God's Word in the power of his Spirit, for the glory of his Son.

Our priorities
Keswick Ministries seeks to serve the local church through:

• *Hearing God's Word*: the Scriptures are the foundation for the church's life, growth and mission, and Keswick Ministries is committed to preaching and teaching God's Word in a way that is faithful to Scripture and relevant to Christians of all ages and backgrounds.

- *Becoming like God's Son*: from its earliest days the Keswick movement has encouraged Christians to live godly lives in the power of the Spirit, to grow in Christ-likeness and to live under his lordship in every area of life. This is God's will for his people in every culture and generation.

- *Serving God's mission*: the authentic response to God's Word is obedience to his mission, and the inevitable result of Christlikeness is sacrificial service. Keswick Ministries seeks to encourage committed discipleship in family life, work and society, and energetic engagement in the cause of world mission.

Our ministry

- *Keswick: the event.* Every summer the town of Keswick hosts a three-week convention, which attracts some 15,000 Christians from the UK and around the world. The event provides Bible teaching for all ages, vibrant worship, a sense of unity across generations and denominations, and an inspirational call to serve Christ in the world. It caters for children of all ages and has a strong youth and young adult programme. And it all takes place in the beautiful Lake District – a perfect setting for rest, recreation and refreshment.

- *Keswick: the movement.* For 140 years the work of Keswick has had an impact on churches worldwide, and today the movement is underway throughout the UK, as well as in many parts of Europe, Asia, North America, Australia, Africa and the Caribbean. Keswick Ministries is committed to strengthening the network in the UK and beyond, through prayer, news, pioneering and cooperative activity.

- *Keswick resources.* Keswick Ministries produces a range of books and booklets based on the core foundations of Christian life and mission. It makes Bible teaching available through free access to mp3 downloads, and the sale of DVDs and CDs. It broadcasts online through Clayton TV and annual BBC Radio 4 services.

- *Keswick teaching and training.* In addition to the summer convention, Keswick Ministries is developing teaching and training events that will happen at other times of the year and in other places.

Our unity

The Keswick movement worldwide has adopted a key Pauline statement to describe its gospel inclusivity: 'for you are all one in Christ Jesus' (Galatians 3:28). Keswick Ministries works with evangelicals from a wide variety of church backgrounds, on the understanding that they share a commitment to the essential truths of the Christian faith as set out in its statement of belief.

Our contact details
T: 01768 780075
E: info@keswickministries.org
W: www.keswickministries.org
Mail: Keswick Ministries, Rawnsley Centre, Main Street, Keswick, Cumbria CA12 5NP, England

Related titles from IVP

Food for the Journey

The Food for the Journey series offers daily devotionals from well-loved Bible teachers at the Keswick Convention in an ideal pocket-sized format – to accompany you wherever you go.

Available in the series

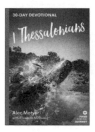

1 Thessalonians

Alec Motyer with Elizabeth McQuoid

978 1 78359 439 9

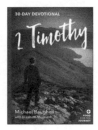

2 Timothy

Michael Baughen with Elizabeth McQuoid

978 1 78359 438 2

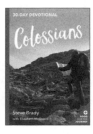

Colossians

Steve Brady with Elizabeth McQuoid

978 1 78359 722 2

Ezekiel

Liam Goligher with Elizabeth McQuoid

978 1 78359 603 4

Habakkuk

Jonathan Lamb with Elizabeth McQuoid

978 1 78359 652 2

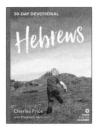

Hebrews

Charles Price with Elizabeth McQuoid

978 1 78359 611 9

James

Stuart Briscoe with Elizabeth McQuoid

978 1 78359 523 5

John 14 – 17

Simon Manchester with Elizabeth McQuoid

978 1 78359 495 5

Available from your local Christian bookshop or **www.ivpbooks.com**

Food for the Journey

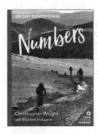

Numbers

Christopher Wright
with Elizabeth
McQuoid
978 1 78359 720 8

Revelation

Paul Mallard with
Elizabeth McQuoid
978 1 78359 712 3

Romans 5 - 8

John Stott with
Elizabeth McQuoid
978 1 78359 718 5

Ruth

Alistair Begg with
Elizabeth McQuoid
978 1 78359 525 9

Praise for the series

'This devotional series is biblically rich, theologically deep and full of wisdom . . . I recommend it highly.' **Becky Manley Pippert, speaker, author of** Out of the Saltshaker and into the World **and creator of the Live/Grow/ Know course and series of books**

'These devotional guides are excellent tools.' **John Risbridger, Minister and Team Leader, Above Bar Church, Southampton**

'These bite-sized banquets . . . reveal our loving Father weaving the loose and messy ends of our everyday lives into his beautiful, eternal purposes in Christ.' **Derek Burnside, Principal, Capernwray Bible School**

'I would highly recommend this series of 30-day devotional books to anyone seeking a tool that will help [him or her] to gain a greater love of scripture, or just simply . . . to do something out of devotion. Whatever your motivation, these little books are a must-read.' **Claud Jackson,** Youthwork **Magazine**

Related teaching CD and DVD packs

1 Thessalonians
SWP2203D (5-CD pack)

2 Timothy
SWP2202D (4-CD pack)

Colossians
SWP2318D (4-CD pack)

Ezekiel
SWP2263D (5-CD pack)

Habakkuk
SWP2299D (5-CD pack)

Hebrews
SWP2281D (5-CD pack)

James
SWP2239D (4-CD pack)

John 14 – 17
SWP2238D (5-CD pack)

Numbers
SWP2317D (5-CD pack)

Revelation
SWP2300D (5-CD pack)

Roman 5 – 8
SWP2316D (4-CD pack)

Ruth
SWP2280D (5-CD pack)

Available from www.essentialchristian.com

Related teaching CD and DVD packs

DVD PACKS

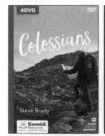

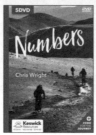

Colossians
SWP2318A (4-DVD pack)

Ezekiel
SWP2263A (5-DVD pack)

Habakkuk
SWP2299A (5-DVD pack)

John 14 – 17
SWP2238A (5-DVD pack)

Numbers
SWP2317A (5-DVD pack)

Revelation
SWP2300A (5-DVD pack)

Ruth
SWP2280A (5-DVD pack)

Available from www.essentialchristian.com